NANCY

A Life from Beginning to End

BY HOURLY HISTORY

Copyright © 2024 by Hourly History.

All rights reserved.

Table of Contents

Introduction
Troubled Childhood
Move to America
The World at War
Becoming the White Mouse
Crash Course in Espionage
Preparing for D-Day
Working with the Maquis
D-Day: Beginning of the End
Postwar Life and Death
Conclusion
Bibliography

Introduction

Nancy Grace Augusta Wake was born on August 30, 1912, in Wellington, New Zealand, as the latest addition to a large family. The sixth child of Ella and Charles Wake, Nancy always had the distinct feeling that she wasn't altogether wanted. Her mother, most especially, always left her feeling that her arrival into the world was more of a burden than a blessing. Nancy later remarked that it was her sinking suspicion that her tired and weary mother had hoped to be done with raising children and that her arrival as a new mouth to feed was not exactly welcome news. She would long remark about how cold her mother was to her and how she critiqued her every action. Her dear old mom seemed to criticize her very being as if it were incumbent upon her to pray an apology to God just for daring to exist.

By her own later recollection, Nancy was raised a God-fearing woman. But the way she feared God in her youth was not what most might consider healthy. Traditionally, the notion that one should "fear God" does not mean that one should be afraid of the Almighty, lest he blot you out of existence. God-fearing is meant to describe someone who has deep awe for God and doesn't want to let down or disappoint God by breaking his commandments. Someone who robs, kills, and destroys with no conscience can be said to be someone who has no fear of God. Someone who is walking down the street minding their own business, afraid that God might strike them with lightning simply because he feels like it, is taking the notion of "God-fearing" too far. It was Nancy's high-strung mother who encouraged such a neurotic view.

This was the suffocating and austere environment that Nancy Wake grew up in. Some might take it as a testament to the Almighty's true love and compassion that she survived it at all.

Chapter One
Troubled Childhood

"My mother . . . was never physically cruel to me or beat me or anything like that, but she gave me no affection, no affection at all. I am convinced she hated to even look at me, and I also suspect that I am an unwanted child by her—that my father came home late one night and had his way, but that she never wanted more children."

—Nancy Wake

Nancy Wake was just two years old when her family made the journey from New Zealand across the Tasman Sea to Australia—to the city of Sydney, to be exact. The move would be full of sadness, however, when her mother and father decided to part company. Charles went his separate way back to New Zealand, leaving Nancy's disgruntled mother to raise the children on her own.

By all accounts, Nancy was a troubled child. According to her own recollection, her only real friends as a little girl were the family cat and dog. She was lonely and often seeking attention—so much so that, on one occasion, she pretended to be pregnant because she thought it would cause people to be nice to her. It sounds ridiculous, and it really was pretty absurd considering that the young Nancy didn't even know what pregnancy was back then. So, how did Nancy Wake get such a strange idea to feign pregnancy for attention?

The whole thing started when Nancy happened to see a neighbor, a certain Mrs. King, who was pregnant. Nancy noticed that big-bellied Mrs. King was treated rather nicely by everyone in the neighborhood. They were sure to ask her how she was doing, if she needed anything, and if they could help her in any way. Affection-deprived Nancy desperately craved this same sort of attention and concern. So, one morning when her mother tried to wake her up for school, little Nancy claimed she was terribly sick. A local physician—a man referred to as Dr. Studdie—was called to see if he could figure out what was the matter with the child.

In private with the doctor, little Nancy promptly informed him that she was pregnant and had him promise not to tell her mother. Although he initially played along, Dr. Studdie wasn't the slightest bit convinced. The doctor was a wise old man and seemed to realize almost immediately that he was dealing with a needy child who was seeking nothing more than attention. He quietly went about his basic examination before calmly informing Nancy that she wasn't pregnant after all. He then had a heart-to-heart discussion with her and inquired with her as to why she thought she was pregnant.

It was then that the truth came out, and Nancy fessed up to the ruse. She informed the good doctor that she just wanted to be treated kindly and taken care of like Mrs. King. The doctor understood Nancy's feelings but explained to the child how she shouldn't use trickery to get attention. Nancy seemed to understand and asked the doctor not to tell her mother of the trickery that she was engaged in. The kind old man agreed, and as far as Nancy could tell, he kept his word since she never heard anyone else make mention of the episode.

At any rate, Nancy's problems only seemed to become magnified by the time she was a teenager. She began to stay out late and even ran away from home on more than one occasion. Nancy herself must have realized at a young age that she needed an intervention. She needed something to set her back on a suitable path and away from the disastrous dead end that she was heading for. Therefore, at the age of just 16, Nancy decided to embark upon a career in nursing. She managed to get hired on as a trainee nurse at a healthcare facility in an old mining town not too far from where she lived.

This was a make-or-break moment for Nancy, which had her making her first attempts at adulthood. It worked out well enough for her, and she stayed on for two whole years. During this time, she learned all the basics of nursing, such as setting broken bones, bandaging wounds, and soothing burns. She also learned a whole lot about life. She had drank, smoked, and hammed it up with a lot of rough-and-tumble men who worked at the mine.

In 1932, after this two-year stint came to a close, she made her way back to Sydney, where she took on a new gig—this time for a shipping company. She was 18 years old at the time and still trying to find her footing. It was in the midst of this transitionary period that she received a fateful letter from Hinamoa, an aunt on her mother's side of the family.

Nancy had heard of this long-lost aunt before in passing, although she had never actually met her. Family members occasionally spoke in hushed whispers about how she had run off long ago, chasing after a whaling captain. The letter was one full of words of rare encouragement and blessing. The aunt had apparently heard of how Nancy had been working hard to turn her life around and heartily approved. The letter was also stuffed with a generous amount of cash to aid Nancy in her efforts to strike it out on her own.

It's not clear if her aunt would have approved of what Nancy did with the money, but as soon as she received this unexpected boon, she quit her job at the shipping company and got a ticket to Vancouver, Canada. This was before widespread air travel, mind you, so this wasn't a plane ticket—Nancy was going to travel by boat. Yes, it's true; she quit her gig at the shipping company, ready to jump ship for Canada. But there was one small problem before she got there—her passport was expired. Since she was still under 21, she needed to have a parent or guardian sign for it.

Nancy had since cut off all ties with her mother, and even if she could work up the courage to speak to her again, she doubted she would ever have approved of her planned sightseeing tour enough to sign for her to get a new passport. It took a moment of consideration, but Nancy soon had an idea. She realized that family doctors were considered acceptable signatures for new passports. It was then that she turned to old Dr. Studdie. Yes, it was the same doctor who had chided her for pretending to be pregnant as a kid. The kindly old man apparently didn't think twice about her request and signed away. Nancy Wake set sail soon thereafter.

Chapter Two

Move to America

"I always took up a dare. I never allowed myself to dwell on the possible consequences of taking up a dare—because that way, I knew I might be scared off—so I usually just did it."

—Nancy Wake

After reaching Canada, Nancy stayed for a while in Vancouver, where she enjoyed the people and the nightlife she experienced. She later described herself as an "innocent abroad," but the truth is she was already fairly worldly for her years. At any rate, after her fun in Canada had run its course, Nancy took transport overland all the way to New York. As one can only imagine, this was quite an adventure for this young woman. It also didn't hurt that alcohol was freely flowing. Yes, even though Prohibition had not yet technically been repealed, New York was awash in drinks and cocktails through various speakeasies, which seemed to almost openly flout the Prohibition laws.

After she had her fun in New York, Nancy made her way to England. Vancouver, New York, and all the rest were just footnotes in her journey; it was Europe where she intended to put down some real roots. Upon arriving in London, Nancy booked herself a room at a local boarding house. She also signed up for classes at a local school, where she took courses in journalism. It's not clear what made her want to choose this field other than the fact that she seemed to think that it would continue to facilitate her keen interest in travel. She very quickly finished up her journalism coursework and was soon offered a position as a reporter covering breaking news in the Middle East.

Back then, even as is often the case today, the Middle East was a veritable wellspring of dramatic and breaking news stories for the news media. Wake apparently laid it on rather thick during her interview, however, and made many impressive embellishments to her résumé. The biggest whopper was when she told her interviewer that she could write in Egyptian.

It's unclear if Nancy was trying to say she could write in ancient Egyptian hieroglyphics, Arabic, or the letterings of the Egyptian Coptic

Church, but her interviewer—impressed by either her credentials or simply her audacity—was inspired to flip the script on Nancy. Instead of hiring her for a role in the Middle East, he offered her a trial gig as a freelance journalist in Paris, France. Here, she would be situated to cover breaking developments in the heart of Europe. It was in Paris that Wake would have a front-row seat to all the developments leading up to the Second World War.

In 1934, a 22-year-old Nancy Wake arrived in the bustling city of Paris. She found Paris to be just as invigorating as she had found New York and London and was eager to embark on an even more exciting adventure. She was soon hitting up popular night spots and making plenty of friends in between the article writing and reporting that her gig as a freelance journalist required her to do. The income she earned from all this was modest, but it was enough. She had enough money to pay her rent, and whatever was left over was carefully used to make the best of France's social scene.

Wake figured that not only was hanging out with the French in their own environment good entertainment—it was also good for business since the more she was able to feel the pulse of the French people, the easier it would be to have an understanding of what was happening around her. This understanding would then enable her to write from a much more in-depth perspective than someone who coldly reported on events with no actual feeling for the people and places that they wrote about. She wanted a front-row seat, and in the nightlife of Paris, that's precisely what she got.

Realizing that there was much to learn about not just French entertainment but also French politics, she soon also began to attend a smattering of political rallies and demonstrations. She didn't want to stand out like a sore thumb during these events, so she quickly learned to dress and act like the French. She wore the latest fashions that the French ladies were wearing, and she even went so far as to get herself a little dog since she noticed that many of the most stylish French women of the day brought a little puppy just about everywhere they went. As such, she got herself a wire-haired terrier she called Picon.

As the political situation in France and the rest of Europe became increasingly complicated in the lead-up to the Second World War, Nancy became convinced that it was in her best interest to learn as much as she could about the political situation on the ground. These early, tentative inquiries inevitably led her to come into contact with the growing movement of the Nazi Party in Germany. France, even at this early stage, was being flooded with fearful refugees who were fleeing from the increasing persecution by the Nazis.

But eyewitness testimony could only do so much. It was in a bid to learn more that Nancy took it upon herself to see what was happening firsthand. She gathered up a group of loyal journalist friends, and together, they made a trip over to Vienna, Austria. The Nazi movement had been growing at a fast pace there as well. Austria had a large Jewish population prior to the Holocaust, and Nancy Wake bore witness to the persecution of this population firsthand during her time there. According to her, it was this experience that crystallized in her mind her desire to do whatever she could to throw a wrench into the Nazi system.

Meanwhile, symptoms of the coming war soon began to erupt all around her. In 1936, the Germans seized control of the Rhineland, a territory nestled in the borderlands of France and Germany. Next, in 1938, they annexed Austria outright. From 1936 to 1939 in the meantime, the Spanish Civil War was being fought just south of

France in Spain. This war featured Nazi-backed fascists of the Francisco Franco regime.

During all this turmoil and international intrigue, there was no end to the stories that Wake could write about as a journalist. She was certainly busy with work, but she still was sure not to neglect her social life. She had been dating quite a few different men at this point, eventually leading up to her meeting and falling for an affluent, older French gentleman named Henri Fiocca. She seemed to truly love this man, though his own family did not so readily approve of her. They were concerned that perhaps she was just after Henri for his money.

Despite their disapproval, Nancy and Henri set the ball in motion for them to get married. As part of their plans, Nancy tendered her resignation from the news company she worked for in Paris, quitting her job with them in July of 1939. She also planned to move from her place in Paris to Henri's in the southern French city of Marseille after the wedding.

Before the wedding took place, however, Nancy wanted to take a little time for herself. She took a vacation in Britain, where she wanted to rest up at a health spa—an activity that was quite popular at the time. During this trip, World War II suddenly erupted. Shortly after she made her way to London, the Germans launched an invasion of Poland, and both Britain and France issued a declaration of war against the Nazi regime.

Instead of resuming her vacation in the midst of this turmoil, Nancy was inspired to head right over to the London news bureau and see how she might be of some use as a war correspondent. However, the British proved to be a bit chauvinistic in comparison to their more open-minded French counterparts. After it was suggested that she might work in a canteen to serve troops, Wake decided to head back to France instead. There, she married Henri Fiocca in November of 1939.

Even though France was ostensibly at war with Germany, there was a lull in the international drama. Yes, Germany had invaded Poland, and Britain and France had declared war, but like chess players observing their opponents, no one was making any further moves at the moment. This lack of action during the early phase of the conflict had many dubbing it the "Phoney War." It all seemed surreal, almost fake. France had declared war on Germany, yet for the time being, life was the same as it always had been. Soon, it would be a much different story when Nancy and Henri's honeymoon was rudely interrupted by the German armed forces and their invasion of France on May 10, 1940.

Chapter Three

The World at War

"The occupation came with bewildering swiftness. One day they weren't there and the next day, they were there in force."

—Nancy Wake

With the war effort fully underway in France, just about all able-bodied men were being called up to join the French war effort. Nancy's husband Henri was included in that general summons. He was drafted in March of 1940. It was then in May that the German war machine bulldozed through the Netherlands and Belgium and on into France from there.

Nancy Wake also wanted to do something to help. She ended up taking one of Henri's cars and converting it into a makeshift ambulance so that she could participate in a volunteer ambulance unit on the frontlines of northern France. Such things were not without precedence. During the First World War, volunteer ambulance units such as this were made great use of. However, the Second World War would shape up much differently than the first one. In World War I, the battlefield of northern France was a stalemate of bloody fighting throughout the entire war. This was not the case in World War II.

Instead of armies being locked in a bloody stalemate in northern France, German tanks launched their so-called *blitzkrieg*, or lightning war, and made such a rapid advance that they tore right through France's main defenses in a matter of not years but days. France was forced to surrender that June. The terms of this surrender were fairly harsh. France ended up losing over half of its territory. The Nazis took over the entire French Atlantic coastline, setting the stage for the later Allied invasion of D-Day.

The rest of France was rendered an ineffectual rump state centered around the southern spa town of Vichy. This so-called Vichy France would be nominal allies of the Nazis, while the rest of occupied France would be directly under the Nazi boot. Since Marseille was within the confines of Vichy France, Nancy and her husband (after returning from the frontlines) were allowed to return to their estate and resume the life they had left off.

But Nancy could not just go back to her old life as if nothing had happened, and furthermore, she became infuriated at anyone around her who meekly decided to toe the Nazi line. She rather quickly abandoned any previous friends who sympathized or even showed the least bit of cooperation with the Nazis. In these perilous times, she realized that she needed to be around a group of like-minded people, so she carefully reorganized her social life to match her own rapidly hardening convictions.

It was from her growing group of new anti-Nazi comrades that Nancy Wake began to become aquatinted with early forms of resistance to the Nazi regime. Some of the resistance was fairly minor in scope, such as simply flying forbidden French flags or vandalizing German wartime propagandized posters. In other instances, the resistance was much more serious, as it pertained to destroying German property or even aiding the escape of refugees out of France. Nancy was in a keen position to help. Not only was she in the know due to her social connections and work as a journalist, but she was also a wealthy woman of means thanks to her marriage to Henri.

Although many other French citizens were way too overburdened to even consider traveling far from their homes, Nancy still had more than enough resources to be able to move about freely. She was also able to use her resources to aid others when it was possible, as she did when she came in contact with a group of British prisoners of war who had been imprisoned at a fortress near Marseille. Nancy did what she could to make the lives of these prisoners easier. She brought them cigarettes, food, and even radios. Such things were incredibly nice gestures during these dreadful wartime conditions—gestures that did not come without their fair share of risk.

And, soon enough, the bold and daring Nancy Wake would do much more than that.

Chapter Four

Becoming the White Mouse

"I hate wars and violence, but if they come then I don't see why we women should just wave our men a proud goodbye and then knit them balaclavas."

—Nancy Wake

As the refugees of the Nazi regime continued to flow into southern France, Nancy Wake found herself at the epicenter of this influx. She wanted to help, and soon, she even went so far as to open up her own home to these political dissidents. She used her chalet, located in Nevache, to provide cover to a large group of them. She sheltered those who were both on the run from the Gestapo as well as the French secret police, known as Milice. The Milice were at times even more feared than the Gestapo since they were entirely dedicated to rooting out French dissidents.

Wake also managed to befriend a British operative named Ian Garrow. Garrow was the leader of a resistance group that would become known as the Pat Line. Nancy soon became a courier of sorts between the French underground resistors and their contacts on the outside and played a pivotal role in setting up safe houses for refugees and escaped internees. Her husband Henri, in the meantime, was helpful by way of his generous financial contributions to the cause. This money was used to purchase food and supplies for those in need.

Food itself was not always so easy to come by during these difficult periods. Nancy often procured her grocery items on the black market. These items consisted of bulk and raw goods. One time, Nancy ordered a whole pig and directed for it to be delivered to her and Henri's home. She later returned home to find a fully living—and distressed—pig tied to a table leg of her kitchen table. Nancy thought that she had ordered a whole, butchered pig and had no idea what she was in for. She had never butchered a pig—what was she supposed to do now?

After giving it some thought, she got the bright idea to hit it over the head with a hammer.

She actually had her maid—a lady named Claire—do the honors, but the blow apparently wasn't enough to knock the beast out entirely. The animal was merely stunned, and so when Nancy tried to finish it off by slitting its throat, it screamed and ran in the other direction. The two then found themselves with a grievously wounded but still very much alive pig, staggering around in their home as it bled from its neck.

Nancy finally took matters into her own hands by striking the pig herself. With some effort, she hit the pig hard enough to finally put it out of its misery. Henri came home and walked right into this bloodbath a short time later. Nancy later recalled how her husband—despite a sarcastic remark or two—seemed to take it all in stride. He knew that he had married a strong, independent woman with more than her fair share of quirks. So did it surprise him that much that she would take the initiative to butcher a pig in their living quarters? Not really.

At any rate, the supply and escape line established by Ian Garrow continued to flow for some time. This situation worked well enough until Garrow was ensnared by the secret police and ended up behind bars. Even so, Wake refused to give up on her friend. She visited him when she could, wrote him letters, and had food sent to him. At one point, she even hired an attorney to stand in court—that is, the Vichy court in southern France—to plead his case. Unfortunately, the attorney couldn't put a dent into the belligerence of the Vichy regime, and Garrow was sent off to a concentration camp.

Nevertheless, Nancy did what she could to help her friend. In fact, she attempted to bust him out of the place. She used her journalistic skills of inquiry to figure out whose palms to grease, and the next thing anyone knew, she had bribed a guard enough to allow Garrow to escape. The money, of course, came by way of good old Henri's pockets, but the execution of the jailbreak was all Nancy. She engineered a plan that had Garrow dress up in a guard uniform, stand in line like a guard, and simply walk out as if it were the end of his shift. Garrow was amazed to breathe free air again and immediately rededicated himself to the cause of the underground resistors. Even so, all of this was not without risk for Nancy Wake.

Rumors began to circulate about a lady who was helping free inmates. At first, the powers that be didn't know that it was Nancy, but eventually, she was indeed made a suspect. But try as they might, they could never find anything entirely incriminating in her behavior. As such, they couldn't find a means to go after her directly. It was the elusive nature of their prey that had the Gestapo refer to her as the "White Mouse." Nancy herself was quite happy that she had been given such a name. She would come to wear it like a badge of honor.

Chapter Five

Crash Course in Espionage

"I started to come to the conclusion that it could only be a matter of time before I was exposed and I would have to be very, very careful indeed."

—Nancy Wake

Big changes were in store for France in the fall of 1942. The Germans had allowed the rump state of Vichy France to maintain its colonies, but after the Allied invasion of French North Africa, the Nazis decided to take matters into their own hands. In November, the Germans rolled right into southern France and began a direct occupation of the territory. This, of course, led to some drastic changes for Nancy Wake and the operations of the underground resistance.

In fact, Nancy sensed that the walls were closing in and decided to make a break for it. She did so by traveling through the Pyrenees Mountains that separated France from Spain and then getting on a boat headed for Britain. Nancy felt horrible over having to leave her husband Henri behind, but she knew that she simply could not stay without being arrested. She had already been held in custody for a few days on her way out of France and was only freed when a friend of hers claimed they were having an affair and her suspicious behavior was due to worry that her husband would find out.

Nancy finally arrived in London in June of 1943. The British capital had changed considerably by this point in time. When she had first landed in London all those years ago, the city was lively and full of all kinds of folks trying to have a good time. Now, not so much. Britain had since survived routine German bombing in what had become known as the Battle of Britain, the air war that was meant to prepare the Germans for an aquatic invasion of the British mainland. That invasion never came since that ever-so-changeable Führer—Adolf Hitler—abruptly changed his mind and decided to invade Russia instead. Even though the British had fended off German aerial bombardment, the signs of damage were there for everyone to see. Both the physical damage of rubble ruined buildings and streets, as well as the damaged nerves of the citizens who endured such treatment.

Nancy Wake hoped that her husband would eventually be able to join her, but in the meantime, she got busy. Initially, she attempted to hook up with the Free French—a resistance outfit of expats working outside France. She was interviewed but ultimately rejected. Nancy wasn't ever really sure of the reason behind the rejection, but she didn't lose sleep over it. Instead, she contacted a British outfit called the Special Operations Executive, or SOE for short. This was a British resistance organization with a special emphasis on undermining the Nazi occupation of Europe. Its so-called French Section was headed by one Colonel Maurice Buckmaster, whom Nancy would come to know very well.

The colonel and his subordinates were busily seeking to probe the depths of German-occupied France in order to find any weaknesses as well as other pertinent intel information. The other objective of the group was to plant partisans on occupied territory who could actively work as saboteurs against the Nazis. Nancy was hired into the group. Her operations were to be strictly confidential, and she would be provided with a cover for her activities. Even while her main task would be espionage for the SOE, she was placed in an entirely different program, the First Aid Nursing Yeomanry or FANY program, as a cover for her work. To the outside world, Nancy Wake would be a nurse, even while she played the part of a daring secret operative behind the scenes and well behind enemy lines.

To get her started, Nancy was trained at a special school just outside of London, which operatives referred to as the "Mad House." It seems that no one could later recall why it was called as such, but Nancy, for one, would later vouch that it was certainly a maddening experience. It's said that she was put through all manner of testing, both physical and psychological. At one point, she was given a Rorschach test, in which a psychologist eagerly awaited her interpretation of a series of ink blots on a piece of paper. People see all kinds of things when presented with this vague bit of stimuli, and that's the whole point of the test. Nancy, however, was not too cooperative with this exercise. She stated that all she could see was a blobby ink blot splashed on the page and simply left it at that. Even so, she passed all psychological tests and exams with flying colors.

Early on during her training, Nancy met a man named Denis Rake. He was a radio operator and an important fixture in the program. The two got along well enough, but Rake had issues with some of the other students. One day, Nancy walked in on Denis when he was right in the middle of a shouting match with one of his trainees. The argument was pretty bad and filled with a lot of foul language. The female trainee on whom Denis had poured his wrath noted Nancy's presence and later approached her and requested that she stand in as a witness for an official complaint. Nancy, however, did not want to get involved. This frustrated the lady to no end, and she ended up complaining to one of the officers in charge, accusing Nancy of being part of the problem. Among the recruit's many complaints, she alleged that Nancy was a chronic alcoholic who drank on the job. This led to Wake being called in for questioning by an officer named Selwyn Jepson.

Nancy was furious at having been called out like this and ended up being very combative with Jepson during his interview with her, which led to her termination. She was upset but unrepentant and marched right out of that office. She arrived back at her apartment in London only to get a telegram requesting her to bring back the uniform that FANY had given her. Nancy fired back a message saying that they could have the uniform back if Jepson himself came and got it and offered her an apology while he was at it. It was at this point that Colonel Buckmaster intervened and made arrangements to get Nancy back into the program.

    He fast-tracked Nancy on a training course in Scotland. Here, she learned the hard skills of the trade. She learned how to handle guns and explosives and was even given a crash course on how to survive in the wild. She was being shaped and molded into becoming a partisan guerilla who could ambush Germans and then melt back into the wilderness to live another day. After this bit of training in Scotland ran its course, Wake was then transferred to a base of operations in Manchester, where she was given instructions on how to use a parachute. Shortly thereafter, she was shifted over to another site, where she picked up skills in using false IDs, conducting reconnaissance, and how to handle being interrogated. It was this bit of training that would eventually make her an espionage agent right in the thick of the action.

Chapter Six

Preparing for D-Day

"We were fairly sure that there would be a tomorrow, but there was absolutely no guarantee that there would be a day after that."

—Nancy Wake

Utilizing her newly learned skills, Nancy Wake jumped out of a plane and floated back onto French soil by way of a parachute in late April 1944. She did this together with 38 women and 430 men who had been sent from Britain to help prepare for the D-Day invasion to come. It was not an easy feat for a few reasons. Number one, of course, there was a steady stream of antiaircraft fire shot up at the plane she had jumped out of. She could have been hit by any one of these bullets. The other hardship, however, was one that she had inflicted on herself.

The night before she jumped, she had partied with other recruits and drunk large quantities of alcohol. Making matters worse, right before the jump, she drank coffee and ate a spam sandwich in an effort to assuage her hangover. This concoction only made the turbulence in her stomach all the worse. As she tumbled out of the plane, she struggled to keep from puking in the respirator she wore.

At any rate, this first phase of the mission was ultimately a success. Nancy's parachute deployed, and she wasn't riddled with bullets. She had a little bit of difficulty coming in for a landing since she ended up getting caught in a tree. Fortunately, some French partisans on the ground located her and greeted her once she found the release chord to her parachute and managed to extricate herself from the tree. She was then led to a main contingent of the local partisan resistance, known as the Maquis.

These particular partisans, although actively working to thwart the Germans, did not have much love for the British and informed Nancy that they were not willing to work with her. Nancy lingered among the group a little while longer and supposedly uncovered a plot on her own life. It's said that she managed to eavesdrop on a conversation of some of the partisans and overheard them suggesting that maybe one of them should try and "seduce" Nancy Wake and kill her so that they could take all of her money and supplies. It was known, after all, that these SOE agents came packed with plenty of resources, and some of these partisans were eager to get their hands on them. As the story goes, Nancy confronted one of the partisans to his face, and he denied that any such thing had ever been mentioned. Plot or no plot—they now knew better than to try and mess with Nancy.

Nancy was eventually referred to another group of partisans that was being led by one Henri Fournier. This particular group proved to be much more receptive. In the meantime, she was reunited with Denis Rake, the wayward radio operator who had decided to join the party. This was crucial since it was Denis who would establish and maintain their communications back to London. That way, they could successfully coordinate a sabotage campaign on the ground with the partisans that would soften up German defenses in advance of the planned Allied invasion.

The Germans would be dismayed to find that many of their communication lines had been sabotaged by these partisans when the Allied forces landed in Normandy, France, on June 6, 1944.

Chapter Seven

Working with the Maquis

"What did I care about trying to be a lady? After what I had been through, the thought that I would worry about whether or not I wore stockings or a hat was completely ludicrous."

—Nancy Wake

By the time Nancy had landed in France, her husband had already been picked up by the German secret police and killed. He perished sometime in 1943, although the exact date of his death is unknown. Nancy herself wouldn't find out about it until after the war was over. So, for all intents and purposes, when she was working with French partisans in the French countryside to sabotage German installations, she thought she was fighting for the freedom of her husband as well as the rest of France.

In the lead-up to the planned Allied landing on June 6, 1944, the partisans in the Auvergne region of France, where Nancy had holed up, were quite active. Soon enough, this activity brought down the wrath of the Germans who were stationed nearby. Matters then came to a head in May 1944 when a large contingent of German troops was sent there in an attempt to root out the rebel French partisans.

The partisans, it seems, had gotten a bit careless in their tactics. In the past, they had made sure not to amass in large numbers in any one spot so as to easily disperse if German forces were alerted to their presence. But they had since amassed in large numbers at the headquarters of partisan leader Gaspard. This attracted enough attention for the Nazis to send in the troops.

It was then, in late May, that the German troops surrounded Gaspard's base and began to engage the partisans. A terrible firefight ensued. Although the French fought courageously, the superior numbers and firepower of the Germans prevailed and ultimately sent the French partisans fleeing into the wilderness. After the smoke had cleared, it's said that some 150 French partisans lay dead. The Allied invasion was getting closer all the time; it was just a question of whether or not the French partisans would survive to see that day.

The other challenge was to keep enough supplies at the ready so that they could be effective at ambushing the Germans all the way to and even during the D-Day invasion. Supplies were regularly dropped from British warplanes that dared to make the flight across Nazi-occupied France. These supplies then had to be gathered and carefully stored so that they weren't ruined by the elements. Any sabotage operations that involved blowing up infrastructure were also carefully timed to match Allied flyovers. This was done in order to trick the Germans into thinking bombs had dropped from the sky rather than having been detonated from the ground. While this worked as a great cover for some time, the Germans eventually figured out what was going on.

In an effort to infiltrate the resistance, the Germans employed double agents. One of these, a guy named Roger le Neveu, was discovered to be a spy and subjected to torture by the French partisans. Nancy apparently walked in on this torture session herself and was horrified at what she saw. According to her later recollection, the partisans were taking turns sticking a red-hot metal poker up the man's rear end while demanding that he answer their questions. If this man had lived, he likely would have suffered terrible debilitating injuries for the rest of his life. But Nancy saw to it that he would not live. In what was perhaps one of the most questionable moments of her career, she encouraged her comrades to shoot the man execution style.

According to Wake, this was an act of mercy since she realized this man was suffering unbearably. Even so, under normal circumstances, it would have been considered an act of cold-blooded murder. After all, this man had even cooperated with them enough to tell them everything he knew—so why kill him? Whether for mercy or for revenge, such random execution-styled killings were fairly common during the war and would often be quickly brushed under the rug by those who witnessed them as just being part and parcel of this terrible conflict.

At any rate, it was on June 5, the eve of D-Day itself, that the partisan groups on the ground received their marching orders. A heavily coded message was beamed to France courtesy of the BBC. The message contained codes about how and where the partisan group should attack German positions. The phrases sounded like nonsense to anyone who did not have a list of all of the special coded words and phrases. Fortunately, Nancy Wake and her group knew exactly what needed to be done.

Chapter Eight

D-Day: Beginning of the End

"We were flat out buggering up everything we could. Everything we could blow up! I was blowing things up all day and night—bridges, railway lines, roads—in no fear of the Germans. This was really what we had come here to do, and now it was a positive joy to do it."

—Nancy Wake

After taking their cues from the radio broadcast, Nancy and company went out all over the French countryside, softening up targets for the impending invasion. According to Nancy, they were blowing up just about anything that would have been of use to the Germans. They destroyed railway lines, roads, and bridges, all of which would make life pretty tough for German reinforcements who would suddenly find their path blocked by rubble.

The partisans usually got away before being noticed by the Germans, but those who lived nearby often suffered the brunt of German wrath. Whole villages were destroyed in some instances as angry Nazis attempted to both exact vengeance as well as gather possible intelligence from the frightened French villagers. "Who did this?" the Germans demanded. "And where are they?" Even if the average French resident could answer these key questions, it likely wouldn't have been enough. The best thing for anyone to do when the Germans came knocking was simply to run and hide. And many did. Many more joined the resistance. It was easier for the average French citizen to rebel at this point, for it was clear to most that the Germans were on their heels.

Then, on June 6, 1944, the Allied forces began their long-planned invasion. After landing on the beaches of Normandy, the Allied troops literally hit the ground running. News of what was happening spread like wildfire among the French, and many more began to join the resistance located in Auvergne. Nancy was tasked with processing many of these ad-hoc recruits, handing them uniforms, boots, and other essential gear.

As the ranks swelled, her group was located by the Germans and attacked. They had been hiding out in elevated, mountainous terrain, only to find that a large German group, complete with tanks and heavy artillery, had surrounded their hideout. The partisans fought heroically to hold the Germans off, as Nancy's comrade in arms, Denis Rake, used his radio to get in touch with their superiors back in London. They were subsequently ordered to withdraw.

Nancy Wake and her group escaped the near encirclement of their camp and traveled on foot for two days with hardly a bite of food and not enough water. It was a very hungry and thirsty bunch who then reached the edge of the town of Saint-Santin. Here, the situation was deemed safe enough to set up camp and recuperate. Since these rebels were often living by their wits on the fringes of civilization, they frequently resorted to raiding the supplies of local villagers. For many, it was deemed a necessary evil since partisans had to eat and drink just like anyone else and often seemed to have no other way to procure suitable supplies. Nancy hated the very thought of stealing from local French villagers, on whose behalf they were fighting. The harsh realities of everyday life and simply surviving to see another day, however, often superseded everything else.

After Denis Rake joined back up with the group, he let it be known that he had discarded his radio out of fear of it being captured by the Germans. This was frustrating for the group since that meant they were now out of contact with their handlers in London. The group soon learned from locals that there was another group of partisans some 125 miles (200 kilometers) away who secretly operated their own radio. Nancy then spoke up and intimated that she would be willing to ride a bicycle to this location.

Many of her colleagues didn't want to take such a risk since the trek meant she would have had to go through many Nazi roadblocks just to get over there. Nancy assured them that she would find a way. Realizing that there was no stopping her, they let her do as she pleased. She hopped on her bicycle and began her journey. Wake took her time and managed to find some rather ingenious detours around most of the roadblocks that had been set up. And after what was quite a harrowing bike ride, she did indeed reach the other group of Maquis. They obliged Nancy's request to contact HQ in London and, in particular, Colonel Buckmaster.

After successfully transmitting her message to her superiors, Nancy then hopped on her bike and made her careful trek back to her comrades in Saint-Santin. She was so weary after biking for days on end that she nearly collapsed when she got to the camp. Nevertheless, after a bit of rest, she was back on her feet. Soon, she and her comrades were once again on the move. They headed north to hook up with partisans under the leadership of French rebel commander Henri Tardivat. Tardivat ordered the group to sit tight in a nearby field that was being used as a drop site.

Along with collecting supplies that were dropped, Nancy also participated in some ambush runs. These ambush attacks were aimed at disrupting Nazi convoys that were racing toward the beaches of Normandy to take on the Allied forces. It did indeed make life difficult for the Germans to have to fend off an invasion, even while getting shot in the back by the partisan rebels holed up in the countryside. The most effective strategy employed was placing bombs along roadsides and detonating them right when the German vehicles passed. The hidden partisans would then open fire on the bewildered convoy as it desperately tried to get away from the chaos that had erupted.

Wake later recalled that the most pivotal moment of this dramatic stand against the

German occupiers occurred when she and her fellow partisans stormed the Gestapo headquarters in the nearby town of Montlucon. This was a carefully orchestrated hit that had the partisans split into two groups. One was tasked with taking out sentries and storming the compound, while the other was left waiting in the distance so that they could return fire at the Germans when the partisans made their retreat. Nancy Wake, for all of her fire and bluster, was made part of the attack group.

According to Wake's later recollection, they used cars to drive to the compound and arrived around 12:25 pm. Wake claimed that she stormed right through a backdoor of the building, ran up a set of stairs, threw open a door, and tossed grenades into the room before closing the door and rushing back down the stairs and then outside. Whoever or whatever was in that command room was subsequently blown to smithereens. Nancy Wake was already back in the getaway car by this time and was hoping to drive right out of there.

The only trouble she and her comrades encountered was crowds of local French citizens who began to block their path. The locals weren't trying to stop them—they actually thought they were being liberated by the Allies.

But in their celebrations, they had crowded the road so badly that the driver of Nancy's car found it difficult to get around these merrymakers. It took a bit of effort to clear them out of the way, but once they did, Nancy Wake and her comrades raced out of there at full speed. They did indeed make a clean getaway.

It was clear by then that the Nazi war machine was being steadily pushed back. Paris itself would be liberated by Allied forces in August of 1944, and the Germans fled Vichy France that September. It was after all this went down that Wake finally learned the truth of what had happened to her husband. He had been arrested by the German secret police in May 1943, and after months of being tortured, he had perished. The Germans had apparently tried to get him to divulge information about Nancy Wake and other rebels, but the stoic Henri steadfastly refused. For this, Nancy would always honor the memory of her beloved first husband.

Chapter Nine
Postwar Life and Death

"I missed Henri, sometimes terribly, and hadn't really met anyone else, but in those situations there is nothing you can do but keep going and that is what I did."

—Nancy Wake

After the war came to an end in 1945, life moved at a fast clip for Nancy Wake. She was given the George Medal, the United States Medal of Freedom, the French Resistance Medal, and thrice, the Croix de Guerre. She was now a highly decorated veteran with a reputation that certainly preceded her. Most didn't know the half of it, but the little they did know was certainly impressive enough.

As the postwar order shaped up, she was given a job for the British Foreign Office, connected to embassies in Prague and Paris.

Before long, however, Nancy Wake felt a growing dissatisfaction with how her life was shaping up. This restlessness is evident from a British newspaper article in *The Star*, where she expressed a desire for more excitement. Working at the British Embassy's visa section, Nancy longed for the thrill of her partisan days. This restlessness eventually led her to leave Paris and return to Australia in January 1949.

When she arrived in Sydney after 17 years away, she was surprised to find herself being hailed as a celebrity, a stark contrast to her anonymous departure in 1932. The headline in the papers read, "Six Medal Heroine Returns," the day she landed. From that moment, Nancy was celebrated everywhere she went. Former classmates and teachers reached out to reconnect, and strangers on the street stopped to shake her hand.

All this publicity and praise prompted Wake to attempt to run for office. She sided with the Liberals and attempted to gain a seat in both the 1949 and 1951 elections. After much fanfare, this celebrated war hero lost her bid to become a politician. Disappointed but not discouraged, she eventually made her way back to Britain, arriving back in London in the year of 1951. Here, she used her war credentials to get a gig with the Intelligence Department of the British Air Ministry. Among her duties was instructing Reserve Units on how to evade capture and escape while in enemy territory. She also focused on creating a comprehensive combat survival manual, detailing the strategies and techniques that had helped her survive during the war.

In 1956, she reconnected with a man by the name of John Forward. John was a fellow veteran who had served as a bomber pilot for the Royal Air Force and who Nancy had briefly met shortly after the war. Nancy and John had a whirlwind romance and soon began talks of marriage. She married him in 1957 and resigned from her post with the British Air Ministry soon thereafter. Eventually, the couple decided to relocate to Australia.

Here, Nancy managed to reconcile with her mother. This was perhaps one of the greatest achievements of her later life. She later admitted that she had perhaps judged her mom a bit too harshly. Her mother was indeed a hard woman to get along with, but Nancy had come to understand that it was her own hard life that had made her that way. It wasn't easy raising a bunch of kids after her husband had abandoned her, and she had become quite bitter about it. In consideration of all of this, Nancy came to acutely understand that old adage about how hurt people hurt people. Her mother was wounded, and she often lashed out at those around her as she struggled to deal with her own pain. Nancy and her husband John would remain close to Nancy's mother until she passed.

Throughout the Sixties and Seventies, John and Nancy enjoyed a happy life filled with friends, cooking, drinking, golf, and long drives. They occasionally traveled back to Europe to visit friends and regularly attended gatherings for Anzac Day and the Royal Escaping Society (a group for Australians who had successfully eluded the Nazis during the war). Journalists frequently interviewed Nancy about her wartime experiences, prompting her to write her autobiography which was eventually published in 1985. The book's success led to a well-received Australian mini-series starring Noni Hazlehurst as Nancy.

In the Eighties, during a visit to Port Macquarie for an air show, John fell in love with the town's charm and suggested they move there for their retirement. They settled into a second-floor apartment, and John quickly adapted to the relaxed lifestyle, making friends at the local veterans' club. However, Nancy still longed for the excitement of Sydney, London, and Paris.

Nevertheless, Nancy's marriage to John remained a happy one, and it only came to an end when John passed away in his sleep on August 19, 1997. Nancy stayed in Australia for a few more years before deciding to once again relocate to her old stomping grounds of London, England, in 2001. She remained in Britain for the rest of her life until she, too, passed away on August 7, 2011, in London's Kingston Hospital at the age of 98.

Conclusion

Nancy Wake is hailed by many as one of the most heroic figures of the twentieth century. Such things might read as hyperbole, but after just a cursory glance at her life, most would likely have to agree with that statement. How many others would parachute well behind enemy lines with nothing but a small pack of supplies and their wits to survive? Time and time again, Nancy Wake found herself in terrible and seemingly impossible situations, but she used her own tenacity and spur-of-the-moment ingenuity to find ways to overcome all obstacles in her way.

Though some have accused her of embellishing her later accounts, it doesn't diminish her legacy. Even if only half of the stories about her are true, Nancy Wake was a real-life hero. She stood up to one of the most atrocious regimes in history, and her life and legacy are a powerful testament to what one can achieve with courage and determination.

Bibliography

Braddon, Russell (1956). *Nancy Wake: The Story of a Very Brave Woman*.

Fitzsimons, Peter (2011). *Nancy Wake: The Gripping True Story of the Woman who became the Gestapo's Most Wanted Spy*.

Wake, Nancy (1987). *The White Mouse*.

Walker, Robyn (2014). *The Women Who Spied for Britain*.

Bernstein, Adam (August 2011). "Nancy Wake, 'White Mouse' of World War II, dies at 98". *The Washington Post*.